BASEMENT TAPE:

COVID-19 POEMS

Richard Stevenson

Cyberwit.net
HIG 45 Kaushambi Kunj, Kalindipuram
Allahabad - 211011 (U.P.) India
http://www.cyberwit.net
Tel: +(91) 9415091004
E-mail: info@cyberwit.net

Acknowledgments

Some of the poems in this chapbook have previously appeared in

Devour: Art & Lit Canada (Volumes 1 &2) and
SciFaikuest

My thanks to the editors for their support of the project.

For Gepke, all she does, all she is...
the best Staycation partner
in any weather. My beacon.

Contents

Various short untitled imagist poems and one concrete poem scattered throughout...

Covid-19

Covid-19's a mean mother,
but ain't from outer space.
Bad hygiene in wet market weather
anywhere: it'll get in your face.

Never mind crossin' genetic lines,
butcherin' and eatin' wild species
in the open air. Piss is everywhere,
waterin' straw and feces.

Now Covid-19 has us in its bite.
Gonna put lotsa folks in lotsa holes.
Gonna spread everywhere overnight,
even to the north and south poles.

(Chorus)

 Covid-19, badass virus
 spreadin' like a grass fire.
 Covid-19, badass virus –
 now we've splashed on gasoline!

Gonna waste our ranks of seniors.
Fill their lungs with sticky gunk.
Give 'em pneumonia, not just flu-like
headaches, chills, sweats, and funk.

Yeah, we gotta take a stacation.
Tromp down its growth curve
to a bump. Yeah, give it less
to chew on. Starve it with a swerve –

A curve of our own right to its
virus glass jaw! Take that!
You stomach content- dwellin'
nasal passage draw.

Gotcha on a crawl.
Gonna getcha on a petri dish.
Settle yer hash. Rain an electron
storm on yo' virus ass.

(Chorus)

    Covid-19, badass virus,
    spreading like a grass fire.
    Covid-19, badass virus –
    now we've splashed on gasoline!

Covid-19, faster than a speeding bullet,
able to jump tall buildings and species.
Smaller than the smallest bacterium
on the smallest rodent's feces.

We gotta starve you of human food.
Let you set in a fridge, unperturbed
while we ping our cells with a new vaccine.
Gonna getcha Covid-19. You and yer herd.

Gonna get yer DNA and mess with it
while yer highjackin' buddies mess with us.

Gonna come up with a vaccine, baby.
Ain't two ways or maybe. Ain't no fungus,

bacterium, virus, or their dreaded spawn
gonna mess with our magnetos,
whether riding on a turd or mosquito bandito.
Gonna trounce you. Bounce you in any weather.

Got it? We're gonna get you. You ain't
gonna vex us for long, however many bodies
you take on the way to yer execution.
Gonna waste you by gosh and by golly.

(Chorus)

> Covid-19, badass virus,
> gonna pull the plug on you.
> Covid-19, badass virus,
> here's *yer* anal port view:

***

doctors now rock stars –
their photos emblazoned on
T-shirts and mugs

*

no ferries or planes –
the harbour taken over
by kayaks and canoes

*

ferries still run –
riders stay in their cars
but for bathroom breaks
guards at washroom doors
enforcing protocols

*

Departure Bay –
even paddlers maintain
safe social distance

*

Easter –
no one on a cross
mugwumps on a stump

*

London Drugs –
masked and gloved *banditos*
both sides of the till

*

fellow masked shopper –
look for eye corner wrinkles
in lieu of a smile

*

before Covid came
Nel had her hundredth birthday
Now she's a shut-in?

*

anti-vaxers
spitting on nurses?!
what next?

*

drive-by shootings, yeah
but drive-by birthday greetings?
not before Covid-19

(for Diane)

*

purebred dogs
cost thousands now –
the price of a lick

Basement Tape

Covid-19 –
good name for a punk/
electro band!

Corona Virus could play
lead in leather
squall in shabby chic

her child-bearing lips could
fellate the microphone
spew raunch and roll

who am I kidding?
punk's done for millennials
rock an afterthought …

might as well form a
geriatric punk band
in my basement

pen some lyrics for
The Prolapsed Colons
(Retired Old Fucks?)

WTF LOL
huge virtual hugs, mo'fo's
I'm on a roll!

***

You-Tube Video

 Covid-19's got Costco
shoppers throwing
 hissy fits

two twenty-something
young women tussle over
shit tickets

a forty-four
magnum roll of two-ply yet
Kirkland brand, best buy!

"one per customer"
Costco has even said "please"
(ladies on their knees)

what? they're afraid to
have to wipe with a hand
or washcloth?!

poor western babies!
in the land of trees, d'ja think
more rolls aren't coming?

still… bill bissett's
"warm place to shit"
resonates now

"Junkies" they said
when Seven Eleven
last turned me down

can't have yellow tape
rope off our place of business
washroom's for staff

now Covid's got the
whole place roped off
nothing's open

can't nip around the
corner to hose down
a dumpster or shrub

what do the women do
in these dire times? no
cars to squat between

homeless can't cage funds
or go on a Stacation
need smack more than masks

a drive-thru lady
stick-handles credit cards
on hockey sticks

they'll be sellin'
shit tickets in the streets
by the yard next week.

***

Body Condoms

I tell you
there's a future
in body condoms

long as you're gonna
wash your feet
with your socks on …

can't do it in a
Hazmat suit
don't look too cute …

yeah, body condoms …
grappling under see-thru wraps
to keep Covid away

***

remember when
safe distance meant six inches
from dress seam to floor?

*

wiping down the buggies
fifty shoppers at a time
could gas jockeys be far behind?

*

insane run on dogs
during lockdown –
returns plug the pounds

 stopped for speeding
cop doesn't ask what's the rush
but are you roommates?

friends fined a grand each
not for speeding, but for
being in the same car

*

shopping in Safeway a masked
customer barks, "you're going
the wrong way!"

stacking the homeless
in steel moving containers –
one solution
currently entertained.
stacking designs, cut holes …

think of the geo-
metric possibilities
cheap insulation,
ease of installation –
just add drugs and stir.

*

hey, I'm 70 –
not a geriatric yet
hear me snore!

*

cardboard crack my son calls
Magic the Gathering cards
sales up, not down

*

anti-vaxers
wave Canadian flags
from the overpass

*

Sasquatch T-shirt:
"Social Distancing
World Champion"

*

the lucky homeless
enclosed in high fences
in steel boxes now

*

think of the gas we're
not burning while
parking our butts and
flattening the curve

*

no water traffic —
crow has the whole bay
to perform acrobatics

*

Anna's hummingbird –
the only species to stay
the winter here
guards *his* feeder by chasing
all other hummers away

in the morning
we find a little corpse
under the feeder.
stabbed or starved? who'd have guessed
birds maintain social distance?

Social Distance

Social distance —
that Newspeak? Euphemism,
oxymoron, or both?

Hey, we're the host and hostess
of the most mangled virus
language ever spat.

We're hip-hoppin' while we
hotfoot across the pandemonium
of pandemics.

Call me on the cell.
I'm always in one at home.
Leave a message on #newnormal.

My web home page is
www.newnormal.calm
to leave a message or spew abuse …

Put your hand in the hand of
the man in silhouette.
Keep you palms wet –

with sanitizer, wise
guy! I'd high five
or bump fists, but no …

Jonesin' on my own,
sittin' by the phone,
more upright than prone.

Hope yer feelin' groovy,
ain't fed up with movies.
Gotta slew. CDs too.

Blue or black and blue –
call the tune to Alexa.
She speaks no Anglish.

Bored games.
Yeah. We gottam. Big fat
juicy cardboard crack ones …

Safeway's spelled out in
stick on arrows – oh,
listen to the sparrows!

Got a gas mask …
Wrong kind? No trunks allowed?
Well, I'm mortified.

Countin' small change, buttons
and belly button lint,
gumdrops in my pocket ...

On forced stacation.
No customers to serve …
No job, Bob Billabong.

I ain't infected,
grade A inspected
stamped past due …

Just another in the
hominid herd
barking with the seals.

All-dressed in blessings,
stocked up in dry goods
cold and flu medicines.

Gonna tough it out
with the over-the-hill gang
make good enough good.

Lay out those
neon red lines. My ass is
parked in overtime.

While in God we trust
in greenbacks we glow
Oh! Don't stop the show!

***

about the homeless some
might say it's God's way of
thinnin' the herd. About such
gormless goofs
God might say *et tu* …

*

how do you flatten a
language virus curve,
find the asymptote of
intention and desire?
what's safe distance between words?

*

mask and gloves – why do
I think my prostate needs
a poke?

*

mask, Hazmat suit
for asbestos removal —
not so good for love

*

talking to himself
a man changes places
before he replies
good listener too:
only replies when spoken to

*

lockdown –
sea lions bark
from closer shores

*

Covideocy

covideocy –
there: a five-syllable word
to describe the act:
ranting about the virus
in absence of the facts

you'd think vidiots would rather
not be seen in such
compromising acts, but, no,
here's one on You-Tube
blaming Corona beer fans –

Mexicans mostly – folks
who prefer bottles to
American cans:
cans the virus won't stick to in
ninety-five degree weather!

we should re-open
the beaches in Jackson,
she says sincerely:
the virus can't take the heat
it bakes evenly, like her

or so she claims.
Can you say Mississippi
without any i's?
How much Coors courage did she
need is what I'd like to know.

***

COVID-19
19-DIVOC
VIDCO-19
19-COVID
DIVCO-19
19 DIVCO
DIV19-CO
IDIV-9CO
D19-COVI
DOVCO-19
OVI19C-D
OVIDC-19
VIDOC-19
CIDVD-19
VOIDC-19
19-VOIDC
VICOD-19
COV-19ID
DIOVC-19
IDCOV-19
IDOV-C19
VOID-C19
ODVIC-19
19ODIC-19
19-ODVIC
VICOD-19
VID-19CO
VOCID-19
19-COVDI
COV-19OI

Covid-19: trumps Trump's
bad news rhetoric now that
we're all mugwumps bathing
in the cathode rays
stuck on a stump

*

Covid-19 got no
vaccine in stores
got fewer stores

*

T-shirt idea:
"too bad governments can't
legislate intelligence"

(thanks Larry)

can't shake hands or
bump fists   can click
heels thrice say over
and over again
there is no place like home

*

haikoodling my wife
calls catching
words viral load

*

bees the size
of hummingbirds are coming
(to a theatre near you)

Departure Bay – no one
coming or leaving
but seals and eagles

*

vaccine passports –
feed your head
not your sphincter

*

humankind –
earth's biggest
viral load

ferries shut down
pleasure cruiser sees how long
a plume he can make

*

defiant punk grrrl has
a 44 bra cup perched
on her beak

*

skull masks?!
not just for movie thieves
or plague goers now

Covid-19 Blues

Buds and birds are
back on the trees;
Still, Covid's got us
weak in the knees.

Can't get to pews to rest
our souls on the foam
and leatherette.
Ain't got no performance goals …

Got the Covid-19 blues.
A need to see some people
in 3-D off the screen,
beyond the virus steeple.

What yellow brick road will get us
from here to Oz? I gotta
scratchy throat and balls, snot
drippin' from a leaky faucet schnoz.

Your know… You gotta know
I got the Covid-19 blues,
head-poundin'-like-a-piston,
no-one-near-enough-to-listen,
lead-foot-with-a-mission blues.

(chorus rejoinder)

Yeah, he's in a fundamental funk.
Got no tiger in his trunk.
Gotta a wider fundamunt.
Stink's now gone to stunk.

Yeah, I got the Covid-19 blues.
Up to the fundament in renos,
investment's plummetin',
lockdown inevitable.
Mugwump sans steno
up to my nose
with rubber hose blues.

Got the—Got the – Got the –
Covid-19 blues. Lead in the shoes,
sunk down to nothin'
mugwump on a stump
gravitatin' Covid-19 blues.

Don't wanna get no fatter.
Still don't want my bones to chatter.
Down to beans and weiners.
Scenery is seener
nothin' seems to matter
Got the – Got the—Covid-19 blues.

***

9 788819 620266 8